FOX
TALES

The Folklore and Natural History of the Fox

By
Brian "Fox" Ellis

Fox Tales International

Presents

FOX TALES

The Folklore and Natural History of the Fox

**Researched, Written, Edited and Performed
by Brian "Fox" Ellis**

**Fox Tales International
P.O. Box 209
Bishop Hill, IL 61419
www.foxtalesint.com**

FOX TALES
by Brian "Fox" Ellis

Table of Contents

SONG OF THE RED FOX

I am the hunter of mice
      yelping on a cold winter night.
I am the one who snatches the cheese
      from the singing crow's beak.
I am the eater of grapes
      because I knew they were sweet
        and I did not give up.
I love hens and will let a few
      grease my chin
         before I leave this town-o, town-o.
And I was not fooled by the lion's complaining,
      feigning illness, to devour my brethren.
You know me as sly, cunning, a trickster,
but did you also know
      that I sang the world into being?
I am friend to coyote
      and can call life back into his limp body
        after yet another fatal mistake.
I am Reynard, I am Zorro, I am Kitsune,
      I am the red fox.
Wise men respect my council.
You, too, can learn from my kin.

SILVER FOX SINGS THE WORLD INTO BEING
A Miwok Creation Myth

In the beginning, when the world was new, all there was was darkness… and Gitchimanitou, the maker of us all. Into this darkness there came a Silver Fox. As this Silver Fox wandered, lost, in the darkness, she felt lonely, so she began to sing:

"Hen-do hi-hi-hi, Hen-do-hi-hi-hi

Hen-do-hey, Hen-do-hey"

As she was wandering in the darkness, singing, far off in the distance, she heard another voice, echoing her song: (Listen and repeat)

"Hen-do hi-hi-hi, Hen-do-hi-hi-hi

Hen-do hi-hi-hi, Hen-do-hi-hi-hi

Hen-do-hey, Hen-do-hey

Hen-do-hey, Hen-do-hey"

And then these two voices began to sing together: (Please sing with me.)

"Hen-do hi-hi-hi, Hen-do-hi-hi-hi

Hen-do-hey, Hen-do-hey"

Silver Fox called out,

"Hey!"   "Hey!"

"Where are you?"   "Over here!"

"Over where?"   "Over here!"

Calling back and forth, these two voices moved closer and closer. Silver Fox found a new friend, Coyote. "Oh, Brother Coyote, it is so good to see you. Let us travel along together so we are not lonely."

As they travelled together, Silver Fox said, "Coyote, let us make a world."

"How do you do this?" Said coyote, "I have never made a world before."

"Neither have I," said Silver Fox, "But let us sing a world into being."

"That's a good idea!" Said Coyote.

So the two of them began to sing together,

"Hen-do hi-hi-hi, Hen-do-hi-hi-hi"

"Hen-do-hey, Hen-do-hey"

As they sang, a small ball of mud began to form under their feet. The mud turned to stone covered with soil and it began to grow grass.

"This is good," said Coyote, "Let us keep singing."

"Hen-do hi-hi-hi, Hen-do-hi-hi-hi"

"Hen-do-hey, Hen-do-hey"

They sang the song of mountains as mountains rose up around them. They sang the song of clouds and rivers and oceans rose up. They sang the song of forests and prairies, fruit and flowers, insects and birds, lizard, bear, and bat. They sang the songs of creatures great and small. They sang the world into being and it was good. It is good.

The people say the world is made of song. They say that if you pause and listen, the world is still singing. They say that if you tune your voice and sing-a-long, you, too, can add to the beauty of this world…

"Hen-do hi-hi-hi, Hen-do-hi-hi-hi"

SIX FABLES FROM AESOP

THE LION, THE FOX, AND THE DONKEY

A lion, a fox, and a donkey decided that if they all worked together maybe they could be more successful. "We each have talents that the others lack, if we put our skills together we can do more," said the donkey.

"Three heads are better than two," said the sly fox. The fox found the food and chased it towards the lion and they caught more game than anyone of them together. The donkey carried the large burden. After a day of hunting, the lion said, "Donkey, divide up the food."

The donkey put the food into three even piles. "Since I have done the division, you can have first and second choice," the donkey said, turning first to the lion and then the fox.

The lion roared his discontent, "You call this math?!" He then promptly devoured the donkey. Turning to the fox he said, "Maybe you can divide this more evenly?"

The fox put the food in two piles, one large and the other small. There was enough for each of them according to their size. The lion smiled. "Your math skills are quite good. Who has taught you the process of division, your management of fractions is superb?"

"Why, I have learned from the donkey;" said the fox, "his example was one not to be followed."

THE FOX AND THE WOLF

Once there was a wolf who was much bigger than any other wolf ever born. He was not only large, but strong and ferocious. The only talent he lacked was intelligence; his brains were as small as his claws were big.

Because he was so large, all the wolves decided to call him "lion." He grew proud. His sense of self soon became distorted. He acted like the king of all wolves. He decided these puny wolves were no longer good enough to be seen with him. He wanted to live with the lions.

A wise old fox who had watched the lion grow up, grow large, and grow big headed, gave him this advice: "You may be large among wolves and king of your tribe, but in a group of lions you are definitely a wolf. Your pride will make you food for their pride."

THE LION, THE BEAR, AND THE FOX

While a lion was silently stalking a wild goat, a bear appeared from nowhere and pounced on the same goat. The lion and the bear argued. The harsh words led to a fierce fight. Claws slashed. Teeth gnashed. Fur flew and blood was spilled. When both were exhausted and wounded severely, they both fell over backwards, unable to get up.

A fox had heard the argument and smelled the fresh meat. He waited, unseen, until the time was right, until they ended their fight. While both of the larger beasts were licking their wounds, the fox dashed in and snatched up the goat. Before they knew what had happened, the fox has disappeared with their dinner.

The lion, licking his wounds said, "Because we each wanted it all, neither of us has the half that we may have deserved."

The bear whined, "The fox has a wonderful dinner though we are the ones who caught it, not him."

The fox, on the other hand, was too busy eating to comment, because his mother always taught him not to talk with his mouth full!

THE FOX AND THE GRAPES

A hungry fox smelled fresh grapes hanging on a vine. Following his nose, he soon found a cluster of fruit dangling from a high branch on a tall tree.

The fox jumped but could not grab them. He jumped again and again, but they were just out of reach. He tried a running start, and leaping from a large rock. He tried throwing small rocks at the grapes but nothing worked.

Finally, he gave up. As he walked away he grumbled to himself, "I am glad I did not eat those grapes. They were probably sour. Who would want to eat sour grapes? They would have left a bad taste in my mouth anyway."

THE FOX AND THE CROW

Once there was a hungry fox, but then again, a fox is always hungry. As he was walking along, he saw a crow with a huge chunk of meat in her beak. This piece of meat was so large the crow was having trouble eating it! The fox thought, "If I could get that piece of meat, I would have no trouble gobbling it down!" He hatched a plan and he set it in motion.

"Oh, there you are sister crow!" said Fox, "I have been looking for you."

Crow eyed Fox suspiciously.

Fox went on unperturbed, "We all know how beautiful you are, the way your midnight black feathers glisten with a rainbow of colors, but I have heard others saying that your voice was a screeching squawk! I defended you, telling them that you had a gorgeous voice that rang out through the forest at dawn! Please prove me right, let us hear your song."

Crow fluffed up her feathers and let loose with a terrific series of CAW! CAW! CAW!

And her chunk of meat fell into Fox's waiting jaws. As he chewed and swallowed, Fox said, "Your voice is fine enough to serve its purpose, but your wits surely seem to be lacking. Thank you for the meat, but next time, try not to be fooled with flattery from a fox!"

THE DOG, THE ROOSTER, AND THE FOX

An old dog could not hunt. He was abandoned by his master. An old rooster whose crow was growing shrill was replaced by a younger rooster. The dog and rooster decided to throw in together, since they were in similar straights. Their first night in the forest, the rooster perched high in a tree and the dog curled up in a hollow log at the base of this same tree. They both settled in to sleep.

When the sun rose the rooster crowed a lovely, loud, ruckus, glad to be free, singing for the sheer joy of it. But all of this noise attracted the attention of a hungry fox. The fox followed his ears until he found the rooster singing to his heart's content. "What a lovely voice you have," cooed the fox, "Please come down so I can meet the master of this beautiful music."

The rooster was not fooled by these sweet words. He guessed the true intention of the fox. The rooster said, "Please knock on that log beside you and you will meet my master."

When the dog awoke he promptly pounced upon the fox. The fox leapt up and ran off. Calling over his shoulder the fox said, "Sorry I must leave so quickly, but your beautiful voice is exceeded only by your wit. It serves you well to stick together, for together you are a brave duet. But alas, I must bid adieu."

All they saw was the red flame of his tail flicker as he disappeared into the dark wood.

THE PRINCESS OF THE FOREST
A Fable From India

A red fox was searching for something to snack on in the forest one day, when all of the sudden a very large tiger jumped out at her from behind a tree. The tiger held down the fidgity fox with only one paw. The tiger was walking in circles inspecting the fox trying to decide whether to eat her or wait for something larger to eat.

The fox knew she could never squirm free, so finally she just stopped trying.

The fox swallowed hard so that when she started to talk she wouldn't tremble. Then she said in a confident voice, "How dare you treat the Princess of the Forest this way? What is your excuse?"

The tiger's eyes opened as wide as apples. He stopped circling. "Pardon me?" asked the tiger, "Are you the Princess of the Forest?'

"That's right! I am the Princess of the Forest," the fox responded. "My mother is the queen and my father is the king. SO I suggest that you do not eat me. If you choose to do so you will be punished in many ways," the fox added.

"Ha, Ha, Ha! I've never heard anything more ridiculous in my life! And besides, if you are telling the truth, and I doubt it, no one has informed me about any of it," said the Tiger.

"Do you need proof?" asked the fox.

"If you do not give me proof, I will eat you," the tiger responded.

"Fine. Let's go," said the princess.

The fox and the tiger strolled together through the jungle. They saw monkeys, elephants, peacocks and deer. Each animal ran away when they saw them coming.

"So now do you believe me? When they see me coming they run in fear knowing that I am the princess," said the fox.

"Yes. Now I believe you are truly the princess of the forest. And I apologize," said the tiger.

They went their separate ways in search for dinner. The fox laughed and laughed all the way home! Because she kept her wits about her, she was able to get herself out of a jam. In cleverness there is great strength.

THE TIGER AND THE FIVE FOXES
A Fable From Pakistan

Not so many years ago, in the forested plains of Pakistan, there lived a mother fox and a father fox with five little baby foxes. Every evening as the market was closing down, they would go to the farmer's market. Not to purchase things as you or I might do, but they would scavenge what was left, hoping to find a small morsel of food. They would feel lucky if they found a spoiled fish or scrap of bone, but more often than not, it was just a few discarded vegetables or crumbs swept from the table.

Every night they would take the same path back to their den. And every night it seems like they had the same conversation, that often went something like this:

"Oh, Mother Fox, how much intelligence do you have?" asked father Fox.

"Oh, about enough to fill a small garden basket," was her answer. But she knew this was her cue to ask, "And Father Fox how much intelligence do you have?"

And he would brag, "I have enough wit and wisdom to fill five large sacks, each sack so large you would need five large oxen to carry them!"

One evening as they were walking home on the same path, having the same conversation, just as these words fell from his lips, out pounced a huge, hungry tiger. Licking his lips, he growled, "AH, ha, ha, ha, I have been watching you! Every night you take the same path but tonight it will be your last, for I am going to eat you!"

Father Fox fainted. But Mother Fox kept her wits about her, what small wits they might be. She said, "Oh, Uncle Tiger, we are so glad to see you." The tiger liked this because Uncle is a term of endearment, and respectful toward your elders.

She continued, "Uncle Tiger, my husband and I have a problem." At this the Father Fox perked up, since he did not know of this problem.

She said, "You see, we have decided to get a divorce." This was news to him!

"And this is our problem: we have five baby foxes and we do not know how to divide them. I am the mother so I think I should get three and he should get two of our kits, but he thinks because he is the father he should get three and I get two of our babies. We cannot decide. Please can you help us, Uncle Tiger?"

The tiger began licking his jowls, thinking maybe he would get to eat all seven of them. When Mother Fox saw this she knew her plan was working.

"I will need to see all five of your baby foxes in order to decide," growled the tiger.

Just as she was hoping. "Father Fox, will you please lead the way back to our home?"

He did not need any encouragement. He leapt up and ran all the way back to their den. Mother Fox took her sweet time, trying not to show how afraid she really was. When she arrived, she turned and bowed to the tiger. "I will only be a moment," she said while backing into their hole, never taking her eyes off of the tiger.

When she got into their den she told her baby foxes what had happened. Then she told them to dig for all they were worth. They dug and dug, down and down, deeper and deeper into the earth.

Meanwhile, the tiger waited... and waited... waited... and waited, growing hungrier and hungrier every moment. By morning he realized they were not coming back. He had been out-foxed! So he slunk off looking for something else to eat.

Meanwhile, the parents warned their young foxes to always be on the lookout for tigers, to never take the same trail twice, and if you see a tiger, it is alright to be afraid...but above all else, you must keep your wits about you.

As for Mr. and Mrs. Fox, they continued to go to the market each evening, and often had a similar conversation. But whenever Mother Fox asked Father Fox how much wit and wisdom he had, he usually said, "Oh, about as much to fill a small garden basket, maybe even, a little less."

THE FOX AND THE ICICLE
An Armenian Fable

A hungry fox was searching for something to eat, and maybe you already noticed, but foxes are always hungry. As he was wandering the forest on a cold wintery day, he saw a large icicle that looked like a bone. CHOMP! He bit into it. He gnawed and chewed. "ARG!" he yelped, "you look like a bone, feel hard like a bone, and even crunch and crackle, sounding like a bone, but not one morsel of bone makes its way into my tummy. You may fool my eyes, my ears, and even my teeth, but you are no bone. I should pay more attention to my gut reaction, you will never fool my belly."

THE FOX AND THE GEESE
A German Fable

A hungry fox was crossing a meadow when over by the lake he spied a gaggle of geese. "Oh, today is my lucky day for there are so many geese I could eat one a day and not be hungry for a month!"

The fox quietly crept along the shore of the lake so he was between them and the water and they could not swim away. He herded them toward a castle wall where they could not fly away and then leapt upon them. "Oh, a few of you are going to grease my chin!"

The geese began to cry out, cackling and honking. They knew they were trapped. They saw their future was bleak. But just then a clever goose piped up, pleading with the fox, she said, "Oh you have caught us all! And it is only right that you eat us all. But please, can I ask one last favor before you devour us?"

"Seems fair," said the fox, "What is it that you want?" "Please promise you will not eat us until we say one last prayer. When our prayers are through and we are right with this world, you can eat us all," said the goose.

"I promise," said the Fox.

One goose began to pray and pray and pray, until a second goose joined in, and then a third, and then a fourth, until soon all of the geese were praying.

Now I would tell you how the story ends, if I knew. But the geese are still praying to this day as they fly away! Do you not hear them? Honk, Honk. Honk!

THE FOX, THE FISHERMAN, AND
THE BEAR'S TAIL
A Norwegian Fable and A Por Qué Story

One day a young man was returning from a very successful fishing trip, riding on his sled which was pulled by a reindeer. He was bragging to himself, "Look at all of these fine fish I have caught. Not only am I the most handsome man in the village, but now I am also the greatest fisherman! Oh, what a good catch I would make." He was thinking about the woman of his dreams and hoping to impress her with this magnificent stringer of fish.

A fox heard the braggart and smelled the fish. He hatched a plan. He ran up ahead and played dead in the middle of the trail. The braggart saw the dead fox and thought out loud, "Oh this fine fox fur will make a fine gift for my one true love!"

He pulled back on the reigns and stopped his sled. He grabbed what he thought was a dead fox and tossed it onto his pile of fish, then continued on his way, continuing to sing his own praise song.

Quietly, the fox chewed through the knot on the stringer of fish and began dropping fish off of the back of the sled. When he had dropped more than enough for a fine feast, he himself dropped off of the back of the sled. The fox picked up each of the fish and headed towards home.

We can only imagine what a fool the braggart must have felt like when he got home and found no fish nor fox fur to give to his sweet-heart. He learned the hard way not to count his fish before they were fried!

As the fox made his way home he met a bear. Bear was surprised at how many fish fox had caught and asked him what his secret was. Fox slyly said, "Oh great bear, it is very easy to catch

so many fish. Let me tell you how. First you cut a small hole in
the ice, then you drop your tail down in that hole. You might feel
the little fish nibbling on the fur, but do not pull your tail out too
soon, you must be patient if you wish to catch as many fish as I
did."

As one may imagine, bear was not very clever. He
thought this was a great idea. And as some may not know, Bear,
at this time, had a beautiful, long, bushy tail, nearly as beautiful
as Fox's brush. So maybe it was jealousy that lead the fox to play
such a trick.

It is easy to imagine what happened next. Bear went down
to the frozen lake. He found a small hole where the fisherman had
recently made a fine catch. Bear dropped his tail into that hole and
waited. He thought to himself, "If I want to catch more fish than
Fox I must wait a long time." As he waited the water froze around
his tail. He mistook the tingling feeling for the little fish nibbling
like Fox had warned him. The next morning he tried to pull his
tail out of the water, but it would not come. He thought he had a
great stringer of fish so he pulled even harder, Harder, HARDER,
until POP! His long beautiful tail broke off!

And from that day until this one, bear has had a short tail,
to remind him of this story, to remind him to be wary of that sly
old Fox.

FIVE FOXY HAIKU

curling up against
the cold of the night, his tail
his only blanket

as the full moon rises
the fox stretches, yawns
little mice, beware

bright eyes staring
into the distance, red fox
looks right through me

red flame of fox
burns brightly this green morning
the flowers nod their agreement

shape shifter, trickster
the one to watch out for is
the fox with a grin

HOW THE RED FOX EARNED HIS BUSHY TAIL
An Original Por Que Story

We have all heard stories of the animals who have lost their tails: how rabbit fell from a tree and his tail snapped off; how bear tried to catch a fish with his tail and it froze in the lake; how possum's vanity lead cricket to clip his thick fur. But here is a story of valor and self-sacrifice, the story of how the red fox earned his bushy tail.

Long, long ago the red fox did not look as he does today, with his bright red fur, black feet and beautiful bushy tail. His fur was a drab, spotty gray and his tail was skinny and hairless, more like a rat's tail than a squirrel's. Oh, he has always been clever and sometimes self-absorbed, but we will get to that later.

One day the fox was hungry and decided to go hunting. Fox was always hungry, in part because he was not a very good hunter. Fox was fast, faster than rabbit, but rabbit could dodge and turn and often got away. He was more clever than mouse, but his drab fur was not the soft red-orange-brown of dried leaves. His distinctive color meant that mouse could always see him coming and slip quietly into her snug little den.

After another unsuccessful hunt, fox sat by the side of a pool of water looking at his reflection. He thought to himself, "I am so drab. I am ugly. I am hungry. It's not fair. I am faster than rabbit but I cannot catch her. Why is it that mouse always sees me coming? Why am I always so hungry? Why am I always cold? I wish my fur would blend in better. I wish I could dodge and turn as quickly as a rabbit." On and on the fox grumbled and mumbled.

As he sat there feeling blue, dwelling in self-pity, drowning in his misery, he smelled something. He smelled smoke.

He thought he heard crackling, yes, he heard the crackling of a fire. Looking out across the meadow he saw a fire raging through the prairie. It was being blown toward the forest, toward his home.

At first he was afraid. "Oh, no! My home will be burned! My wife and children will be scorched!" Then he thought about all the other animals whose homes would be ruined, all the lives that would be lost. Even his nemesis the rabbit might lose her life; her resting place under the bush was already up in flames.

As the fox began to think about something besides himself, as he began to think about his family and the other animals of the forest, a new feeling came over him. He was no longer afraid. He felt a new kind of bravery. He knew he had to act.

Quickly, he ran out in front of the fire. He began stomping on the flames. The fox shrieked and shouted as loud as he could, "Run! Run for your lives! There is a fire in the prairie and its burning toward the forest!" As he shouted he continued stomping on the fire. It was not working. His feet were not big enough, but he was clever and his heart was growing to match the quickness of his mind. The fox dropped to his side and began rolling across the fire, extinguishing the flames.

The animals heard his warning and all of them escaped. Their homes were ruined for now, but they knew that the prairie and forest would renew themselves. The flames actually enrich the soil; the ash is fertilizer and you must clear away the old to make room for new growth. When the flames had died down and the animals returned to assess the damage, they were stunned to see the fox lying there scorched and dead.

Or was he? As the creatures of the forest gathered around, they saw him slowly take in a breath. It was actually the mouse who said, "Look he's still alive! I felt the air come out of him."

As the animals stood in silence, staring, the rabbit whispered a prayer. The rabbit knew that it was the fox who kept her fast, it was the fox who kept her alert. As her kin feed the fox, the fox kept the warren healthy and strong by eating the old and sick. And some day the fox will die, adding his bones to the dust that helps the grass to grow, to feed the rabbit, but that day was not today. With these thoughts in her heart, the rabbit whispered a prayer, "Please Creator, save him as he saved us."

Just then a gentle breeze blew a whirlwind of dust and ash that seemed to sparkle in the sunlight. Before the astonished eyes of all the creatures the fox began to sprout new fur, not the drab gray he grew before, but a fur that was brilliant orange and red like the flames they had seen just moments before. His feet and legs sprouted black fur like the ashes the fox had stomped so bravely. And then he grew thick fur on his tail to help him dodge and turn and to keep him warm on a cold night. His wishes had all been granted.

Soon a healing rain began to fall across the forest and fields. New life sprouted everywhere. The mouse and rabbit quietly slipped away knowing they would be chased by a better hunter. The fox slowly stood up. He looked at himself in the nearest puddle and knew that these new gifts were given because of his valor.

To this day, the fox has a bushy tail to help him dodge and turn, to keep him warm on a cold winter's night. He has red-orange fur to help him blend in well with the dried leaves and grasses of the prairie and forests. And the red fox has black feet to help him remember this story, to remember the time he risked his life to help those around him.

FOX WENT OUT ON A CHILLY NIGHT
An Old English Song, Popular in Modern Bluegrass!

Fox went out on a chilly night,
he prayed to the Moon to give him light,
he had many a mile to go that night
before he reached the town-o, town-o, town-o,
he had many a mile to go that night
before he reached the town-o.

He ran till he came to a great big bin
where the ducks and the geese were kept therein.
"A couple of you will grease my chin
before I leave this town-o, town-o, town-o,
a couple of you will grease my chin
before I leave this town."

He grabbed the grey goose by the neck,
threw the goose over his back;
he didn't mind the quack, quack, quack,
and the legs all a-dangling down-o, down-o, down-o,
he didn't mind the quack, quack, quack,
and the legs all a-dangling down.

Old Mother pitter patter jumped out of bed;
out of the window she cocked her head,
Crying, "John, John! The grey goose is gone
and the fox is on the town-o, town-o, town-o!"
Crying, "John, John, the grey goose is gone
and the fox is on the town!"

Then John he went to the top of the hill,
blew his horn both loud and shrill,
the fox he said, "I'd better flee with my kill
He'll soon be on my trail-o, trail-o, trail-o."
The fox he said, "I'd better flee with my kill
He'll soon be on my trail."

He ran till he came to his cozy den;
there were little ones eight, nine, ten.
They said, "Daddy, daddy, better go back again,
'cause it must be a mighty fine town-o, town-o, town-o!"
They said, "Daddy, daddy, go back again,
'cause it must be a mighty fine town."

Then the fox and his wife without any strife
cut up the goose with a fork and knife.
They never had such a supper in their life
& the little ones chewed on the bones-o, bones-o, bones-o,
they never had such a supper in their life
and the little ones chewed on the bones.

"SO, FOX, HOW DID YOU GET YOUR NAME?"

This is the question that I am most often asked, so several years ago I put together a performance of stories that begins to answer this question. This book includes all of those stories and more. I began with the beginning of the world and told a creation myth about a fox singing the world into being; the world is made of song. I wove in a fox fable or two or three. I sang a fox song and recited a poem or two. I then told stories about my family tree and my Great Uncle Johnny, who was half Cherokee and had a pet fox. Only at the end of the hour did I tell a personal story about my pet fox and the dream in which I was given my name.

All of this to say: ***Who we are is a collage of family stories and cultural cosmology.***

I was thinking this was a clever and original idea, until I was deeply humbled and amazed to find that Geronimo had done the exact same thing when interviewed for his biography one hundred years earlier. He began with a creation myth, told of his tribal and family history and only at the end told his smaller story within the context of his culture's larger story. The Cherokee author of <u>The Witch of Going Snake and Other Stories</u>, Robert J. Conley, created a fictional "Biography of Yellow Bird" that also began with a creation myth, covered the trail of tears and ended with just a few paragraphs of this man's existence. Black Hawk, too, began his autobiography with several pages about his family tree, his grandfather's vision and his tribal history. These Native American authors could not separate their individual lives from the ongoing story of Creation. What I have done with this book echoes a long tradition.

This tradition of seeing ones' self in this larger context is ancient and yet somehow missing from our modern understanding of the Self. Yet our Creation Stories are an integral part of our personal narrative.

What is our personal story in light of our cultural history? How do our parents and great-grandparents still influence our choices? How does our cultural belief system color our daily decisions? How can we act as the hands and mind of Creator? What are the future implications of today's actions? How will our lives influence the next seven generations? (If you can answer any one of these questions please let me know!)

What I do know is this: It is through our stories that we know this larger self and our place within the cosmos. It is through our family stories that we keep our ancestors alive. Simon Ortiz, a Pueblo storyteller, once told me that our creation myths say more about us than they do about creation, yet the world may not be fully made if we do not tell these stories.

Please talk to your elders and collect your family stories, before it is too late…

MY UNCLE JOHNNY AND HIS PET FOX
A Family Story Infused with Family Folklore

Fox is more than a nickname. I was given this name many years ago. But when it was new, my Great Aunt Irene gave me a copy of this 1880's photo of my Great-Great Uncle Johnny Clanton. She was a little girl when he was an old man, but she knew him. He had a pet fox and chose to have his picture taken with this young fox and his favorite fox hound, Tennessee Belle. They say a good foxhound was worth something. Maybe that is why my uncle chose to have his hound dog in the picture with him, knowing that back in those days a picture was a rare and expensive luxury.

I was talking to my Aunt Irene about this picture. She told me that my great uncle was born and raised in Wayne County, Tennessee, near the home of Davy Crockett. My father was born on that farm, eight miles from Davy Crockett State Park. Uncle Johnny's mother was Cherokee, her name was Hannah Jane Reed. He was also related to the Clanton Clan who faced Doc Holiday and Wyatt Earp in the famous shoot out at OK Corral, but as usual, Hollywood got that story all wrong, or at least that is what my Aunt Irene used to say.

When people remember Johnny Clanton they would always say that he was a great hunter. I have mixed feelings about hunting, especially fox hunting, but my Aunt Irene assured me that they never killed the fox. It was a game of wits. In the evening, the men would gather with their hounds. They would build a big fire and sit around listening to the hounds chase the fox. If something happened and the hounds did not come back, a man could leave, leave his coat by the fire, and when he came back in the morning, his dog would be sitting by the coat waiting for him.

Now I grew up fishing and hunting, but I never went on a fox hunt, so I can only imagine what it was like based on the stories I have heard. Imagine with me.

Just before sunset my Uncle Johnny would whistle up his favorite hound. The two of them would wander down the ridge to the pasture by the edge of the woods. There may be two or three other men with their favorite hounds, but sometimes it was just my Uncle and Tennessee Belle. There might be a fire if it were a cool night or a low smokey flame to keep the mosquitos away if it was warm. There might be a mason jar of spirits passed around with the quiet conversations. When it was dusk dark, the talk would grow still as the hounds were turned loose. My Uncle Johnny would lay back and listen. In a quiet holler you can hear many things echoing in the distance, a whip-poor-will along the creek bottom, the last whistle of a bob-white in the high meadow, the first hoot of a bard owl, who-cooks-for-you, who-cooks-for-you, who-cooks-for-you-aaalll.

But what he was listening for was the bawl of hounds. After a while they would hear a few sharp barks and know that the hounds had found the scent and off they went. The barking would increase as other dogs picked it up. Then there would be a long bawling howl and they knew the scent was fresh. The sound of the hounds would grow more faint as the fox lead them up over the ridge. It would grow quiet for a while before the howling came back over the other side and circled around to the south. "Ha, that ol' Mr. Fox was leading them up through the barn yard and out towards the horse pasture," Uncle Johnny would mutter to himself or no one in particular. Then the hounds began yipping and yapping, and you could hear the confusion in their voices. Their barking moved back and forth a few times, before Tennessee Bell's unique howl rose above the confusion. "That a girl!" Uncle Johnny would murmur. He knew right were they were …

"Why that old fox must 'a jumped up onto the split rail fence and walked the top fence rail for awhile before he came back down, losing the pack of hounds in confusion. But he couldn't fool my Tennessee Belle, she found the place where he jumped down off that fence!"

Hours passed as the fox circled the valley a few times leading the hounds this way and that, playing games with the dogs to the delight of the old men laying quiet in the fresh mowed field of the lower pasture. It was a theatre of the imagination, listening and knowing. Occasionally there would be a chuckle, a whispered praise for a hound, or even an admiring bit of poetry for that old Mr. Fox. The men often said he seemed to enjoy the challenge as much as the hounds. If they did not run the dogs now and then, Mr. Fox would come scouting round the barn as if he was taunting the hounds, daring them to spend a night on the hunt.

Jut then the barking grew louder, closer and louder, louder and closer still. The men sat up and watched. Sure enough, that ol' fox came right down the valley along the edge of the creek right towards them. In the moonlight, he saw the men and they saw him. He seemed to nod his respects and they nodded, too. Then that ol' fox feigned to cross the creek. He jumped out onto a few rocks jumping around to leave his scent real strong so the nose of those ol' hound dogs would think he was just there. Their excitement would get in the way of their thinking and they would spring on across the creek running on off up the ridge. But that clever fox went back into the water and walked down stream a long ways so the dogs would never find his scent. He had his sport, but he was getting tired and decided to call it a night. He headed on home.

The dogs did just as ol' Mr. Fox expected them to. They raced across the creek and headed up the ridge. It wasn't long before their barking grew confused. A few dogs came back down to the creek and began to go back and forth trying to pick up the scent. But they never found it.

Uncle Johnny had had his sport, he too, was tired and decided to call it a night. It was quite a show that night. He whistled up his hound and he and the other men headed home. "Until we meet again," he whispered to Mr. Fox, "until we meet again."

SEEING THE WORLD WITH WILD EYES
The Story of My Pet Fox

When I was a kid, our house was a zoo. Even though we lived in a big city, near downtown, we often had more than 100 pets including several wild animals!

We always had at least five dogs and when they had pups we could have as many as fifteen. My dad raised blue ribbon hunting dogs. He trained them to hunt and sold them as a way to make a few extra dollars. We often had as many as a hundred tropical fish in eleven fish tanks. My dad had a friend who owned a pet store and we sold fish to the pet store. I tell you, my house was a zoo.

Once, my brother and I bought my dad a pair of finches for father's day. Within a year my dad had 100 mated pairs of finches! For a long time he raised Gouldian finches from Australia. These birds are day-glow colors in the wild. My dad started cross breeding them with simple Mendelian genetics and was able to get colors that never existed before! These birds had purple chests, red faces with a black circle around them, greenish-yellow backs and orange bellies. Did I tell you? My house was a zoo!

We raised bobwhite quail that we let loose in the wild to help repopulate this native bird. At different times, we had a pet raccoon and a pet squirrel. We raised chickens for eggs. My mom had a potbellied pig. And my brothers and I brought home the usual assortment of frogs and toads, snakes and salamanders, turtles and mice.

We especially loved bugs! We caught fireflies on warm summer nights. We hatched praying mantis eggs for our garden. They eat lots of bugs that eat our food. We had an ant farm. We caught caterpillars and raised them into butterflies, but we always turned them loose when they were ready.

My favorite pet of them all was a red fox.

My dad had been out coon hunting with his brothers, my uncles. One of the dogs found a dead fox by the side of the road. A car had hit the fox. The fox was still warm. But that wasn't the saddest part. The saddest part was that it was a lactating vixen, it was a mother fox with milk, which meant that somewhere out there in the woods were baby foxes without a mother.

The men put all of the dogs on leashes, except John Boy. He was an award winning hunting dog with the best nose in the business. John Boy picked up the scent of the fox and followed it back to the den. The kits, or baby foxes, were in a big hollow log. My dad crawled into the log and came out with three of the tiniest baby foxes you could imagine. Two went to my uncles and one came home with my dad.

By the time they got home from hunting it was four o'clock in the morning. My dad woke up my three brothers and I. He said, "Boys, come here. I have a surprise for you in the kitchen."

When I walked into the glaring light of the kitchen, rubbing the sleepiness from my eyes, I was amazed to see this little bundle of red fur. It was the cutest creature you could imagine. It had the sweetest face: round eyes, round nose, and small rounded ears. Its eyes had not even opened yet.

My mom had four babies of her own so she had lots of baby bottles. Mom warmed up some milk and put it in a bottle. Then she handed it to me. I had seen her feed my baby brother, so I knew to put a small drop on my wrist first to make sure it wasn't too hot. It was warm but I didn't flinch, so I knew it was just right. I loved the smell of warm milk. My dad handed me the tiny bundle of fur. I cupped the kit fox against my belly and put the nipple in her mouth. She was obviously very hungry. She suckled, gulping down the warm milk. The fox kit opened her eyes and looked into my eyes. We stared at each other, lost in that moment.

When a baby feeds, whoever is feeding the baby is seen as its mother. I felt like the baby fox's mother. She looked at me as if she were my pup. In that moment we connected and I began to see the world through wild eyes.

My brothers and I argued at length about what to name our pet fox. We made a long list of possibilities. We finally decided on the most creative, original name we could imagine… NOT! We named our pet fox Foxy. How plain.

Foxy grew up fast. We had lots of adventures together. I could tell dozens of stories about her. Let me tell you three:

One morning I came down to breakfast in my pajamas with bare feet. My mom had made some hot oatmeal for breakfast. As I was standing in line with my brothers waiting for my oatmeal, Foxy was walking around my feet. I wiggled my toes and Foxy pounced on them! Ouch! I got an idea. I wiggled my toes on the other foot. She pounced on those toes. Ouch! She would pounce on my toes and I would jump. Ouch! But as I lifted one foot she would pounce on the other. Ouch! Faster than I could jump from one foot to the other Foxy would pounce back and fourth. This was a really fun game… while she was little, but as she grew so did her claws and her teeth. Ouch! Oh! Ow!

In that moment she showed me that even though we thought of her as our pet, she wasn't. She was a wild animal with instincts that would help her make it on her own. Playing at pouncing was how a wild animal practices what she needs to know to survive in the wild. From the beginning my dad told us, "A wild animal does not make a good pet. She will be much happier running free." So we knew that eventually we would have to let her go. Our hope was that she could fend for herself. She was showing us that she was quick, quicker than we were. As I hopped from foot to foot she would pounce on the other foot before I could lift it! Ouch! Oh! Ow!

That summer, my brothers and I went to a day camp at the local city park. One day they announced a pet show and told us we should all bring our favorite pet and they would give us prizes. Lots of kids brought their dogs and cats. A few kids brought gerbils, hamsters, and birds in cages. One girl even brought her goldfish in a glass jar. It was one of those speckled goldfish with big, round eyes. But we were the only kids in town who had a pet fox.

We put a little green collar on her and walked her like a dog on a leash. Of course she won best of show. We received the biggest red, white and blue ribbon. Everyone loved that she was smart, social and playful like a dog, but a little aloof and independent like a cat.

My oldest brother, Bruce, a teenager, was holding the leash after the pet show. He was talking to this foxy girl, showing off, and he was not paying attention to the four-legged Foxy-girl. Nearby was a great big German Shepherd who was growling at Foxy. Foxy was not afraid. She was pulling on her leash, inching over closer to this big mean dog. My brother was not paying attention. All of a sudden the dog lunged at Foxy, growling, barking, and foaming at the mouth. But Foxy was so suave, so cool. She dropped back on her hind legs, just out of reach of the German Shepherd and as quick as any boxer she reached out and slapped the dog on the nose with her sharp little claws. That great big dog yelped and slunk away, a coward, his tail tucked in between his legs. He was afraid of our little Foxy and her lightning quick jab!

In that moment, Foxy showed us she was no pushover. She was brave and quick. She showed me that the old saying was true, dynamite comes in small packages! And maybe, maybe she could take care of herself; maybe she could make it on her own in the forests and fields of her natural home. As summer was winding down we knew that she would soon be turned loose to roam wild on her own.

To help her with the transition, and because my mom was tired of Foxy chewing up the legs on her furniture, tearing up the pillows on the couch, and leaving little smelly presents under the bed, we put Foxy outside in one of the dog pens. She climbed out the top, so we put a fence over it. She dug a tunnel under the fence, so we filled the holes with big rocks. She dug around them, so we put her on a leash inside the dog pen.

She still dug out under the fence and quickly learned how long the leash was, how far she could go. Luckily for her it was a long leash because she would hunt in the tall grass behind her pen. There were little birds that visited the tall grass and took dust baths in the alley behind our house. The sparrows would rub their chest in the dust to rid their feathers of mites and lice. The finches would eat the seeds of the tall grasses and weeds. I know because I would watch Foxy hunt. I would watch her watch the birds.

I loved to watch her hunt. She would quietly crawl under the fence and sit perfectly still in the tall grass. Of course the birds would fly away when they saw her coming. But she would settle down to wait and her mottled red fur blended in beautifully with the brown and reddish-yellow of the dried grasses. She would sit still as long as it took for the birds to forget she was there. I, too, would sit perfectly still and watch.

As I watched I began to imagine what it would be like to be a fox, to have red fur, sharp claws and teeth, a bushy tail. I began to see the world through her eyes.

Eventually, the birds would come back, tentatively at first. But it wouldn't be long before they would begin to take dust baths, fluffing their feathers and stretching their wings without a care in the world. At this moment, when the birds least expected it, Foxy would pounce. But she did not leap straight at the birds; she was smarter than that. She knew that birds could fly. She would leap into the air above the birds. She would turn herself around mid-air so the birds flew up into her. When she landed, she landed on a bird.

She would have more than feathers for lunch!

She knew just how long the leash was, how high she could jump. She could not only predict the flight path of the birds; she could direct them with her pounce and maneuver herself mid-air to intercept them. She caught so many birds that she stopped eating her dog food and began to cache or hide some of the extra birds so she could eat them later.

Of course we helped a little by putting bird food on the ground behind her pen and raking the alley for the perfect dust bath. We may have helped to lure them in, but it was Foxy who caught them.

We now knew that Foxy could feed herself. She was quick. She was brave. And she was a great hunter. She was wise enough to store extra food for leaner times. At dinner our family discussed how and when to turn her loose. We all agreed that she would be happier in the wild, yet we would be sad to see her go.

I would like to tell you that this story has a happy ending, but to be honest, I'm not sure how the story ends. There are parts I can only imagine.

One of the last weekends before school started our family typically went camping one last time. We often went to my uncle's lake house in western rural Ohio and camped on the shore of Lake Diane. We got our neighbor to feed and take care of our pets while we were gone. When we got home Foxy was gone. She had chewed or torn the fastener where the chain linked to the fence.

We looked high and low but could not find her. There was a huge swamp in my neighborhood, "undeveloped wetlands" between two rivers. The marsh was surrounded by junk yards, a toxic waste dump, project housing, factories, a prison and my neighborhood. We thought, we hoped, that she had found her way into the marsh and could make a go of it there. We knew there were other foxes there and plenty of mice, rats, snakes, berries, and little birds for her to eat.

I did see Foxy in an alley on my way to school that fall. She had knocked over a garbage can and was gnawing on a bone. I knew it was her, because not many wild foxes wear a little green collar. When I called her, she looked at me like she knew me, like she was tempted to come. She thought about it, but decided to take her bone and run. She was now more wild, more wary.

We caught glimpses of her several times that fall, but she never came when we called. As fall turned to winter we saw less and less of her. I must admit that we were most worried about her making it through the winter. Northern Ohio winters can be harsh. There were frequent blizzards and sometimes a whole week would pass and the temperature was not above zero.

The next spring I was playing in the marsh with some friends. We climbed a great big oak tree overlooking a large meadow. From the top of the tree you could see the skyscrapers of downtown Toledo, the Maumee River, and the smokestacks across the river. My best friend Chip saw the foxes first. He tapped me on the shoulder and pointed. I don't know if it was Foxy for sure, but there were two foxes frolicking together. I yelled, "Foxy!" and they both looked up at us for a moment before they ran away.

I would like to think one of them was Foxy. I would like to imagine that Foxy and her mate raised a litter of kits that spring so long ago. I still sometimes imagine that the children and grandchildren of those foxes are still living in my old neighborhood, but I don't know for sure.

I will tell you what I do know. I still carry a picture of Foxy in my wallet. I love to pull out the picture and look into her eyes. I remember all of the adventures we had, all the things I learned from her: to be quick and brave, to take care of yourself and put a little extra away for leaner times, and most importantly, through her, I learned to see the world with wild eyes.

FLYING FOX DREAMS
A Dream within a Story, A Story within a Dream

When I was a little boy, my grandma told me that we were part Cherokee and she looked it. Though I now know it was a small part of my genetic make-up, we are mostly Scots-Irish and German, with a little Polish and Viking. Like many Americans we are mutts, part Immigrant and part Native. I might be more junk-yard dog. I grew up in the city, Toledo, Ohio, with smoke stacks and factories, sky scrapers and a junk yard in my neighborhood. But I always felt like we lived in the country, hound dog. We raised chicken and quail. We had a pet squirrel and a pet raccoon. We even had a pet fox. We always had half a dozen dogs. We grew most of our food, canned and froze what we grew, hunted and fished for the rest.

As a boy I loved the adventure tales of Daniel Boone and Davy Crockett. I read every book I could find about American Indians. As a boy scout I learned as much as I could about wilderness survival. At 17, I ran away from home… to live in the woods … to go to college. I swore then I would never live in a big city again and except for a few years while my girls were young I have kept that promise to myself.

After my first year at college I had a choice. I could work at a fast food joint flipping burgers or I could work at a summer camp where I would get paid to play tag and go fishing. For me that was an easy choice! I went to camp. For the next ten years I was a camp counselor and that is how my storytelling career began. And every year since I have told stories at summer camps for more than 40 years!

It was at this time that I decided I needed to know more about my Cherokee ancestry. I went to live with my grandma for her last year of life, to take care of her and to gather her stories.

I also began to go to lectures and read more deeply about Native history and culture. But learning about your culture from reading a book is like learning to swim without getting wet. It was about this time that I met an Ojibwa Elder named Sun Bear. He grew up in Minnesota, worked as a stunt man in Hollywood, and then dedicated his life to preserving and passing on Native Wisdom. He published a few books. He had a vision that told him to organize Medicine Wheels, to bring together elders from many nations to share their knowledge. Those who knew of him, might have heard that he was a controversial man, but I knew him well, and I would say at least some of the controversy was for the right reasons.

He invited me to travel with him as he organized large Medicine Wheel Gatherings where as many as a thousand people would come out, people from over the world, to share what they knew and help us all reconnect with the ways of our ancestors. There were African Yoruba Priestess, Hawaiian Kahuna, Chinese Herbalists, and Elders from many Native American Nations. And there were stories told around the camp fire every night. This is where I learned the craft of a good story, well told. For almost ten years, during the spring and fall, I would travel the Medicine Wheel circuit, in the winter I would travel to schools as a storyteller, and during the summer I would return to summer camp.

There was another camp counselor who had worked at this camp a few years before I got there, David Sharpe. Every time someone told me anything about him, how he used to do this or that, they would say something like, "Oh, if you knew David, you and he would be best friends!" The next summer David returned. When I first saw him get out of his car and come dancing into the campground, I walked right up and said, "And you kind sir, must be David Sharpe." He stopped in his tracks, looked at me as if to say, wha.. how.. who are you?

But before he could speak, I told him how everyone at camp last summer said that he and I would be best friends. They were right. That first night we stayed up into the wee hours of the morning swapping stories and songs. We decided since the camp tents were not up we would grab our sleeping bags and sleep out under the swirling stars, dancing around the fire that is the North Star, just as we had earlier in the evening danced around this smoldering fire. Circle dances were a tradition at this camp.

It turned out that David was a dancer and pantomime who wanted to learn more about storytelling. So we spent much of the summer swapping skills, he helped me with the physicality of storytelling and I helped him with language and poetry. We became fast friends.

But that first night, after I told him I had to go to sleep, five times, he turned to me and said, "Two words."

"Fox, you are a fox, Flying Fox!" Then he rolled over and we both went to sleep.

At first I did not know what he meant. Oh, I knew the fox was a trickster. I had been collecting stories about foxes since I had a pet fox. I knew that the fox was respected around the world, sly, clever, tricky. Every culture tells fox tales because foxes live on every continent. (Yes, I know they were introduced to Australia by the English, who also brought their fox tales with them. In Mexico, Zorro means fox. Fuchs in Germany, Kitsunami in Japan, Reynard in France. I know foxes. My favorite line was and still is: "You better watch that fox, he might trick you … into learning something!"

These were some of my thoughts I might have had as I slipped into slumber that night.

Did you know that you dream every night? You often have 3-5 dreams, but rarely do you remember any of them. But then there is that rare and wondrous night when you have the most vivid dreams. You wake up for a moment and wonder to yourself, was it a dream? Because it felt more real than the waking world. Pay attention to those dreams. That night I remembered three dreams:

In the first dream I was in my old neighborhood, in the North End of Toledo, walking down the street, when a friend pulled up in her car and stopped. I leaned into the window and we chatted. I don't remember the conversation. What I do remember was watching this little boy, about 8 years old. He came walking down the sidewalk like any other eight year old, and then turned to go in between two houses. When he crossed that invisible line into the shadows, when he thought no one was watching, he did a silly dance, like something Elvis might do on stage to win the hearts of his adoring fans. My friend and I both laughed out loud! I loved that boy! I was that boy…

The dream changed.

In the second dream it was a dark night, nearing day light. I was in a casa de carton, a house made from a cardboard box, like I saw when I lived in Mexico and in the bigger cities of the United States. I was homeless, again. I was curled up, half asleep, dreaming within my dream, that I was part fox. I had a snout and bushy tail, with patches of fur on my human skin. I was stuck in transition half-way between being a fox and being a human. I twitched. I ached. I knew I better change back into a human before the sun rose. This did not feel strange to me, like I made this transition every night. While the world slept, I wandered the city streets as a fox. Not quite a panic, but I felt the urge to change back into a human quickly or I might be stuck in between worlds. Part of me would rather be a fox than a human. I felt like I had this dream often…

The dream changed.

In the third dream, I was myself, at camp again. I was coming back from a three day expedition into the wilderness. There were a dozen of us, kids and counselors, and we were singing. We were tired and hungry and dirty and smelly, but we were really happy. It had been a great camping trip!

To get into camp we had to cross a rickety old swinging bridge made of rope and wire with wood planks. Because of weight restrictions, only four people can cross at a time. The counselor at the front and three kids crossed. The next four kids crossed. The last three kids and I bringing up the rear began to cross. I paused on the bridge to look down into the flowing water. The kids who had crossed earlier were playing around in the bushes and spooked up a fox.

The fox ran up onto the bridge. It was running straight towards me! It was a narrow bridge. I made my arms and legs into a sort of basket as if I were going to catch the fox. It jumped up, swerved and wiggled through my arms and legs to run down the other side of the bridge. I was closer to the other end and jumped down. The fox was running along one side of the river and I along the other.

Just then I heard hound dogs barking and I knew why the fox ran so furiously.

Then the fox ran out onto a rock in the river and danced around to leave its scent quite strongly. It jumped onto a second rock and third, each time dancing around to strengthen its scent upon the rock. Them it jumped into the stream and swam downstream before getting out on the same side. Clearly an effort to fool the hounds!

I quietly cheered as I continued to follow the fox along the opposite shore.

Then the fox turned to cross the river. It began running straight towards me. Its first few footfalls were on top of the water. Its next few foot steps were in the air slightly above the water. Its next set of foot steps were in the air! It was flying! It was running and flying straight towards me! I opened my arms to catch it! As I wrapped my arms around it, it flew straight into me! Into my chest, my heart! The fox became a part of me…

And I woke up…

When I woke up, I sat up for a moment, remembering all three dreams in the quiet dark of that morning. I sat there stunned, feeling how real it all felt. That fox is still a part of me…

And from that moment on, I knew what my name was. I have been Fox ever since, and maybe long before…

THE FOX DEFINES EVOLUTION'S TERMS
Natural Selection at Work in the
Foxes of North America

Charles Darwin, growing up in England, only knew the red fox. When he was a college student, he met John James Audubon. He marveled at Audubon's paintings of birds and mammals. And Audubon's travels in North America inspired Darwin's travels around the globe. As he travelled the world, he was introduced to other species of foxes.

Later in life, while Darwin was working on his book <u>On the Origin of Species</u>, he was also on the board of the London Zoological Society. The Hudson Bay Company gifted Audubon's son with a black fox that lived in his apartment while he lived in London. It was later given to the London Zoo. All of this to say, that if Darwin would have known the foxes of North America, they could have helped him to better explain his complex idea of evolution.

Evolution is easier to understand if you remember these key terms: **V.I.S.T.A. = Variation, Inheritance, Selection, Time,** and **Adaptation**. Darwin's concept, his VISTA or point of view, is best defined by these five words.

The **Variation** of species via the **Inheritance** of specific traits, through the process of natural **Selection**, over a broad expanse of **Time**, allows the **Adaptation** of individuals to evolve into new species.

Variation – Within a species there are slight differences between individuals; these differences are called variations. For example, if you were to photograph a hundred red foxes, you would notice that some have fur that is more orange than red, some are actually black, and some have a color pattern that looks like a cross on their back. Some might have shorter legs or longer legs, smaller ears or larger ears. These slight **variations** might allow some foxes to thrive and reproduce while others would be more likely to get eaten by a predator or they might have trouble catching their food. They would not survive and pass on those weaker traits to their offspring.

Inheritance – With two parents, each parent gives half of their genetic material to their offspring creating a child, (or seed, or egg). This includes traits from both the mother and father, yet the offspring is unique. The kit fox, or baby fox, that is born with longer legs inherits this trait from his parents. But in a family of foxes maybe only two inherit this trait, maybe two foxes have longer legs and two have shorter legs. Nature would select the traits that help that individual survive and their offspring would inherit those traits.

Selection – Because there are many more offspring born than the natural world can support, some who are more fit to survive will thrive and create their own family. Those less fit will die; no offspring inherit their traits. In this competition for food and shelter, in this struggle to eat and avoid being eaten, nature selects the fittest. Natural selection is also called the survival of the fittest. So, the foxes with longer legs are better able to catch food and run away from their enemy on the open prairie, while those with shorter legs might be better fitted for climbing trees. Over time one family who has long legs runs faster and the family with shorter legs climbs better.

Time – Long stretches of time, thousands of generations are required for new species to arise. But time is relative. For viruses and bacteria who reproduce dozens of generations in a few days they change, adapt, evolve much more rapidly than elephants, which take 22 months to give birth. But over the course of dozens of generations, individual species can slowly change to create new species. One red fox living in a desert will not change her color or grow larger ears to help her survive in this hot, dry climate. But over great periods of time and many generations, her great-great-great-grand-daughter might adapt, evolve, and slowly change into a San Joaquin Kit Fox, especially if there is a mountain range that separates this group of foxes from all others so their gene pool is limited.

Adaptation – As the earth changes, as climates change, animals change. These slow gradual changes are called adaptations. Eventually these adaptations, these gradual changes, add up and new species are created from the old. As foxes with long legs move out onto the prairie, their offspring with longer legs thrive, produce young, and this adaptation leads to a new species, the swift fox. As they move into the desert, those with larger ears, those who are smaller, better able to release heat and regulate their temperature, will thrive. They produce young who inherit this trait and over great expanses of time, the desert fox evolves. Gray fox fur is great camouflage if you also have short legs for climbing trees.

In North America we have several species of foxes, all distant cousins to the red fox. Each have adapted to their unique environment. Longer legs help the swift fox catch its food and avoid its predators in the open terrain of the short grass prairie. Larger ears help the desert fox evaporate heat. Gray foxes have shorter legs and are the only fox that regularly climbs trees. These Adaptations, over great expanses of Time, have allowed these foxes to survive through natural Selection, so the traits are passed on to their young, Inherited, and what was once just a Variation within a species has eventually led to several new species.

This is what the Fox Says:

Through time, species adapt to their environment. And through natural selection, new species arise.

You can choose any family of creatures: mammals, insects, trees, flowers, birds, or worms, and you could write a similar short essay that uses the five key terms and explains how evolution has shaped different species within that family.

RED FOX REVISITED

I am the swift one.
I have sharp ears
for hearing voles digging
under a foot of snow.
I have a keen nose
for sniffing out danger
and avoiding the dogs on the hunt.

I can fly higher and faster than the quail,
leaping and twisting,
pouncing on my lunch.
I am the runner, the digger, the leaper.
Mice shiver when they hear me yelp.
Vixen melt with my caress.
I am the hunter, lover of life, caring father
and guardian of the forests and fields.

The prairie burns with the red flame
of my swishing tail,
often all you will see of me,
if you are lucky enough
to catch a glimpse at all.

But you should know that I am watching,
always watching you
when you enter my terrain.
You should know that I,
I am the red fox,
and I know the hidden trails of my domain.

SING A FOX SONG!

The fox is a popular creature in folktales, songs and poetry from around the world. He is Zorro in Mexico, Kitsune in Japan, Reynard in France, Brer' Fox in the African American tradition, and Tsula among my Cherokee ancestors. Aesop wrote more tales about Fox than he did any other animal. Fox is always sly, clever and she often outwits her enemies. In part, because I had a pet fox when I was a boy, I have collected fox stories and poems as long as I could read. I have also written a great number of Fox Songs!

What is your favorite wild animal? Make a list of short phrases that tell me what it looks like. Make another short list of colorful phrases that describe what it does/what it is good at/ what is its role in the wild world. Make a third list of the titles and phrases that give us the synopsis or the moral of the story from all of the folktales you can find about your favorite animal. Use these lists to create several poems: one more scientific like the last poem in this book and one more allegorical or fable like, like the first poem in this book. You could spell out the name down the side of the page and write an acrostic poem or write several haiku that add up to a longer poem, like "Five Foxy Haiku" in the middle of this book. But, instead of a fox song you might be singing a bear song, or a fish song, or a snake song! What is your favorite wild creature? Sing your own song!

FOX FABLES CHART

Each of the animals in Aesop's Fables has well defined characteristics. For example, the fox is sly, witty, and a trickster. Make a list of five or ten of your favorite animals from the stories you have heard. Use this list to create a chart that defines each animal's strengths and weaknesses. Then, use this chart to write your own fables!

Characteristics:

Make a list of positive and negative characteristics, adjectives that describe characters: Vicious, mean, cruel, lazy, kind, compassionate, huggable, slow, fast, smart, dumb, clever, gullible, _______________, _______________, _______________, _______________, _______________, _______________, _______________, _______________, _______________, etc.... (Use these words and others like them in your chart).

Next, make a list of your favorite animals. Begin this chart on your own and then ask friends and family to help you complete the chart.

Animal	Positive Traits	Negative Traits
1. Ex: Fox	Clever, Observant	Sly, Deceitful
2.		
3.		
4.		
5.		
6.		
7.		

Keep this chart and use it to write many fables. For now, put a star next to your favorite animal, the one you want to be the star of the story. Put a circle by another animal, who will be the supporting actor, best friend or enemy, in the tale. Write two sentences about each animal: one sentence that describes what the animal looks like; and one sentence that describes the animal's characteristics. Use words from the chart to help you with your sentences.

Setting: Setting is less important in a fable. In a ghost story the setting is critical, but in a fable the ecosystem of the animal is the normal setting. Write two sentences about the place where the story takes place. Describe the habitat , the home, of the creatures involved. What plants and animals share its home? What is the weather like?

Plot: Using a classic idea of human virtue and good behavior, create a problem and solution that exemplifies this characteristic. You could tell a tale that models the right choice or create a story that shows what goes wrong when you don't make the right choice, a cautionary tale. Create an outline for your story:

1. Beginning
   2. Problem
3. Middle
   4. Solution
5. End

And the moral of the story is:

The Story: Use the chart and these sentences as the raw material. Tell your story to a friend. After telling your story, write it down. Edit and rewrite your story. Then share the story with your friends and family!

POR QUÉ
or
How and Why Stories

Many cultures tell animal stories that seek to understand the life and times of our animal friends. Though we know this story is fantasy, there is a lot of good science in this type of story. What parts are true? What can you learn about nature reading one of Aesop's or Tolstoy's fables? If you study traditional folktales they include a lot of ecological wisdom. You can write your own Por Qué story.

A Por Qué story explains why an animal has a certain trait, like how did the chipmunk get his stripes? Or how did the eagle get his white head? Or why does the raccoon have a bandit's mask? Or how did the bear lose his tail?

Choose one of your favorite wild creatures. Write a brief description of its unique characteristics. How does it look today? Write a brief description of how it once was before it changed. How did it change? Draw a before and after picture of your creature.

Describe the animal's habitat including information about weather, food, shelter, landforms and other plants and animals who share its home. Think of a problem it may face. How does it solve the problem? What does your animal learn from its mistakes and successes?

Answer these questions and use this information to write your own Por Qué story! (Use the boxes on the next page to doodle and jot down ideas)

Before (plus or minus one key trait)

After (what the animal looks like today)

ABOUT THE STORIES & THEIR SOURCES:

- "Song of the Red Fox" is from my book of the same name, (Fox Tales International 2003)
- "Silver Fox Sings Our World Into Being" is a Miwok story from Northern California that I learned when I lived there. My favorite version is by Joseph Bruchac in Keepers of the Animals, (Fulcrum 1991)
- Six Fables From Aesop can be found in most good collections, but An Argosy of Fables edited by Frederic Cooper includes many fables from around the world. (Stokes 1921)
- "The Princess of the Forest" is also in An Argosy of Fables.
- I learned "The Tiger and the Five Foxes" for a program at The Field Museum; there are several versions online.
- "The Fox and The Icicle" is an Armenian Fable by Vardan of Aygek, 1180-1250, later published in The Fox Book, printed in 1668 in Amsterdam, also in An Argosy of Fables.
- "The Fox and The Geese" is from the Brothers Grimm. My favorite translation is by Jack Zipes (Bantam Books 1992)
- "The Fox, The Fisherman, and The Bear's Tail" is a mash-up of two stories; both have Norwegian and Native American versions. See Swedish Folktales and Legends (University of Minnesota 2004) or Iroquois Stories (Crossing Press 1985)
- "Five Foxy Haiku" are original and not published elsewhere.
- "How the Red Fox Earned His Bushy Tail" is also in my book Learning From the Land, (Libraries Unlimited 2012)
- "The Fox Went Out On A Chilly Night" is a children's book by Peter Spier (Double Day 1961) and a song by Nickel Creek (Sugar Hill 2000) - there is also a version from the 16th century!
- "My Uncle Johnny" is a mostly true family story with a nod to The Education of Little Tree by Forrest Carter (University of New Mexico Press 1986)
- "Seeing the World Through Wild Eyes" is autobiographical.
- "Flying Fox Dreams" is as true as any dream was ever true.
- "The Fox Defines Evolution's Terms" was adapted from my book Charles Darwin and his Revolutionary Idea, (Fox Tales International 2020).
- "Red Fox Revisited" is also from Song of the Red Fox, (Fox Tales International 2003).

Brian "Fox" Ellis is an internationally acclaimed author, storyteller, historian, and naturalist. He has worked with The Abraham Lincoln Presidential Library and Museum, The Field Museum, and dozens of other museums across the country. He has hosted, produced, written, and researched several documentaries for PBS and has recently launched a podcast titled, Fox Tales International. He is the author of more than 2 dozen books including the critically acclaimed <u>Learning From the Land: Teaching Ecology Through Stories and Activities</u>, (Libraries Unlimited, 2011), a series of Chautauqua style autobiographies, History In Person series, and this collection of Fox Tales Folklore. Many of his stories are also available on his YouTube channe,l Fox Tales International. He and his wife run a Bed and Breakfast in Bishop Hill, Illinois, The Twinflower Inn, where he also leads bird watching adventures!

Devin McSherry is a freelance illustrator, hand-lettering artist, and surface pattern designer born and raised in the Prairie State of Illinois. Her best days are spent walking through nature, illustrating things that inspire her, cooking from scratch, and keeping her hands busy with sewing and other crafts. She's also learning to garden and enjoys getting involved with local permaculture-focused organizations. She currently lives alongside her husband, Ryan, in the suburbs of Chicago. Are you interested in working with Devin on your next creative project? You can view more of her work and get in touch by visiting her website (<u>www.devinmcsherry.com</u>) and following her on Instagram (@devin.mcsherry).

Vin Luong (DEC), born in Vietnam, was the son of widely known Chinese painter, Sui Hong. He studied traditional eastern technique and classic western art. Blending these two styles he created art that was at once realistic, surrealistic, Asian and abstract.

**This Book is part of a Multimedia Series Available at
<u>www.foxtalesint.com</u>
Visit this website to see the other books in the series.**

**If you purchased the audio book
and video here is your access code:**

**To watch a performance and listen to more
Fox Tales Folklore
in this series you can also subscribe to
the YouTube channel and podcast:**

Fox Tales International